FOLLOW YOUR DESIGN

(Re)discovering your Truth and Purpose

Damon,
May this book inspire you on your journey as your perseverance and wholeheartedness inspire me!

Michelle Layli Farnsworth

Michelle Layli Farnsworth

Cover Art: Michelle Layli Farnsworth
Author Photo: David Henderson

Follow Your Design: (Re)discovering your Truth and
Purpose
Copyright © 2021 by Michelle Layli Farnsworth

For information contact us at:
https://www.mainspringfoundations.com

Instagram : follow_your_design_rediscovery
FaceBook : Follow Your Design Official Book Group

ISBN: 978-1-7368988-1-9

First Edition: April 2021

For my daughter Karida.

May this book inspire you
as you have inspired me
since the moment of your birth.

Thank you for choosing me, Dida.

My Truth

Through my writing and art and conversations and deep inner work I find patterns for deep transformation on every level. I have found a connection with the spirit world and the physical world that assists me with my pattern making from the center of my core. I am amazed each day at what I learn, and remain ever curious. It is a blessing to know my Truth.

My Purpose

I am able to bless others through sharing my pattern making for deep transformation. I share it with the world in ways I can currently imagine, and those I cannot yet and stay open to Spirit guiding me. I am amazed each day at what my heart and soul perceives, and my body and mind translate into patterns for the benefit of all. It is a blessing to live my Purpose.

Welcome!

You were guided to this book because you are looking to deepen or strengthen your journey to find your Truth and Purpose. I pray this may be of some assistance and that you feel my love for each of you through my words.

-Michelle

CONTENTS

Beginning

I have been guided and blessed over the last 15 years to have completely transformed my career, health, relationships, and finances and healed from my past traumas. I now live in a place of gratitude and ongoing learning. I have struggled with codependency and people pleasing, with remembering to use my voice and my power, with overthinking and analysis paralysis, with trusting the Universe/God to guide me, with remembering who I am instead of who the world wants me to be, with remembering to love myself and lavish myself with self-care, with falling for the negative voice in my head, and with remembering to trust my intuition. Some days I still struggle.

Thankfully, the work gets easier and easier over time as I continue to remain committed to my growth and learning and have more tools to draw from. Now I have more days than in the past when I am living in my authentic self, fully in my power and intuition and living out my divine design. I believe my divine design is to help others through coaching, courses, and my writing to reclaim their authenticity, power, and inner knowing, to discover their own purpose and truth and live it. I provide the questions and the space to explore, and I believe that you already have the answers inside of you.

Our work together - whether through this book, in private coaching sessions with me, or through the courses or retreats that we at Mainspring Foundations hold - is about overcoming the things that get in the way of you living your authentic life (fear, expectations, 'should's, mental blocks, etc.).

I am a partner with you, and I know that you have the strength and wisdom within you to make it happen. My goal is to create a space where you can tap into your own intuition to powerfully guide your decisions.

What I share is my personal experience, tools I've relied upon in my own journey of healing, my intuition and what I've seen that helps my private coaching clients. In this book I share much of what I've learned as I have tapped into the connection to the Divine for inspiration. I trust that when we work together, everything is possible.

This book can be read in the order presented or you could skip around or read it backwards or see what pages or chapters you are drawn to read each time you pick it up. Some chapters have questions or potential practices at the end that you may wish to reflect on. Or not. The importance is to follow your own intuition always, whether about how to use this book or the decisions you make in the rest of your life.

This is my gift to you, and I hope it brings you clarity, truth, purpose, direction, and peace.

A few notes:

Throughout the book I use the Universe/They/Them to speak of the unknowable Divine essence Who created and cares for us. Please feel free to replace this with God, Goddess, Allah, Jehovah, the Almighty, the Great Spirit, Energy, Love, or whatever resonates the most with you, even if it is nothing at all.

I also use they/them to refer to the Noble Self. I see this part of each of us as our soul, which I believe has no gender. Feel free to replace they/them with a gender if it resonates better with you.

L I S T E N

If we could be guided by the abundance of our Noble Selves, we could create an entirely different world.

I've come to understand that each of us are composed of two parts: a Noble Self and a Shadow Self.

The Noble Self is what some call soul, spirit, intuition, higher nature, or heart. It's the part of us that is connected to something greater than ourselves and the part of ourselves we connect with in meditation or moments of wonder or happiness or peace. The Noble Self is the essence of certainty that has an inner knowingness, a belief in abundance, and a trust in the greater forces at play.

The Shadow Self is also known of as the ego or lower self. It is the part of us that we were given to protect the Noble Self. It has an important role to play as the protector. It was created when we were small children trying to make sense of the world. It is fueled by fear, a belief in lack and a need to control.

When we have conversations in our heads or conflicts of what to do, it is really a conversation between the Noble Self and Shadow Self. For most of us it is the fear-based Shadow Self who we tend to listen to more. It is the more insistent self and more prone to tantrums, and so we tend to give into it. In moments of clarity, we all have had a chance to listen to our Noble Self, but most of us forget to pay attention because the Noble Self's voice is much quieter.

Ask yourself who you'd rather was guiding your life? The abundance-based Noble Self or the fear-based Shadow Self?

This is a tricky question because immediately the Shadow Self will jump up and say, "ME"! But see if you can wait a bit for the quieter voice of the Noble Self to see what they say. You may need to pause, breathe, and wait for that voice to speak. They aren't used to being heard so take your time to just listen.

And wait.

What do you hear?

Your Shadow Self will probably be jumping in again, saying, "I've got this, I've always protected you against the world." Ignore that self or maybe lovingly say, "Yes thank you for everything you do for us, but I'm curious to see what the Noble Self has to share. Let's both listen together."

And listen.

The Noble Self's voice comes through in different ways: it may be words, but it also may be a feeling in your body of calm, memories of happy moments, smells that remind you of a favorite person in your life or your favorite food your grandmother used to cook, or promptings to call a certain friend or open to a certain page in a book.

They give us guidance much more subtly than the Shadow Self, so we have to learn how to listen. We have to create quiet spaces in our lives to hear. We have to build trust with our Noble Self so that they speak up more and commit to hearing and following their guidance.

Most of us, without realizing it have let our Shadow Self guide us for most of our lives. It's not our fault, it's what we know, what we were taught. It's how society is structured, leading us to believe that we have to figure out life on our own, in competition with each other. But it doesn't have to be this way. If we could be guided by the abundance of our Noble Selves, we could create an entirely different world.

LIGHTNESS

I am light
I am love
I am life
that is all I've ever been

Sometimes it is life
that obscures the light
that confuses the senses
and delays the faculties
that tricks us into believing
that life is light when it is not

Light is in those moments
of darkness when we do not
believe we can ever
come through

Light is in those flashes of clarity
that we try to hold onto...
but can't

Light is in the pain and betrayal of all

that we once thought
was pure and true

Light is in love lost and
found and lost
and found again
Light is in the darkness;
that is its true power
that is its Divine essence
that is its supreme joy
that is its culmination

Light harnesses the power of darkness
and the two ride
together

That is true life
That is true love
That is true light
I am life
I am love
I am light
that is all that I have
ever been
and all that I
will ever be.

TRUTH AND PURPOSE

Our Truth and Purpose is something we understood innately as children and along the way most of us have forgotten. It's time to (re)discover it.

The most important thing is to understand that we are on this earth for just a short time. This may sound trite or overused but it is true.

We were put on this earth for a Purpose and to share a Truth and we must be faithful to that mission. The core of the mission is determining what your Purpose and your Truth is in a world that has placed labels and stories and narratives around who you are to be, since birth. Our Truth and Purpose is something we understood innately as children and along the way most of us have forgotten. It's time to (re)discover it.

I use these two - Truth and Purpose - seemingly interchangeably, but they are not the same.

I see Truth as the energy of knowingness, intuition, flow, connection, and power. I see Purpose as the energy of doing, action, completion, structure, and strength. Each us have both energies in us.

When we live our Truth, we are in touch with ourselves, our intuition, our knowing, and the flow of life and open to Guidance. When we live our Truth, our energy is more calm and generative, our relationships with friends and family are more nurturing and non-judgmental, and our inner world is more at peace.

When we live our Purpose, we are doing, creating results, and in action towards something bigger than ourselves. When we live our Purpose, our energy is more directed, our relationships with friends and family are more supportive and protective, and our inner world is more at peace.

Most of us live with purpose where we are active, getting things done by being productive. Living with purpose (instead of living our Purpose) means that where we spend our time may have been chosen by others, to impress others, or to fit in with the norms of the society we live in. We can spend decades living with purpose, which can bring some value to ourselves and others. But at some point, we may lift our head up and realize that something is missing. It is our Purpose.

Most of us do not live in the flow and intuition of truth (much less our Truth) as we are told that the most important thing in society is to be productive. Most of us were not taught to understand ourselves, to follow flow, or to listen to our intuition. We spend our lives grinding each day to be productive and can spend decades doing this. But at some point we may lift our head up and realize that something is missing. It is our Truth.

All of us must (re)discover our Truth and our Purpose and learn to balance the two. A beautiful analogy is to consider Truth as a beautiful river and Purpose as the banks of that river.

Truth brings the content of who we are, how we are, what qualities we bring, what we create in moments of intuition, and how we stay connected to the world around us. Our Truth is our river that flows with no specific form or direction except to flow. Our Truth is always present but at times can be high or low depending on the season or how much we have remembered to recharge ourselves through self-care. Our Truth is life sustaining for us and others in our world.

Purpose brings structure to how we are in the world through our work, what we produce, and how we bring value. Our Purpose are the banks of our river of Truth that provide direction. Our Purpose channels our Truth to benefit ourselves and others. Our Purpose moves our river of Truth towards an end goal. This goal could be uniting with other rivers in a larger body of water to bring greater Truth to the world, or sharing your Truth with those in your close vicinity. Once you know your Truth you will know what your Purpose is.

If your river of Truth doesn't have a river bank of Purpose to direct it, it would just be a large puddle of water that could flood and destroy the land. If your river banks of Purpose don't have a river of Truth to direct it , it is just dirt and stones with no purpose.

We need both equally.

We need to know when to act and when to wait. When to speak and when to listen. When to push forward and when to let things lie for the time being. When to work and when to rest. When to be accountable and when to be compassionate with ourselves and with others.

What is your Truth?

What is your Purpose?

NOBLE SELF

"...the body can discern, to the finest degree, the difference between that which is supportive of life and that which is not."
-David R. Hawkins, M.D., Ph.D.

The Universe only wants your happiness. It wants your joy. It wants you to live a life equal to your power as a loved creation of God.

In life it is important to look for what is meant FOR you by the Universe, not only to know what to stay away from.

Your Noble Self, connected to the Divine, guides you when you listen. The voice of your Noble Self may be quiet. But don't mistake their quietness for weakness – they are powerful and are aligned with the Divine in each moment. They will tell you how to be and what to do in this next moment, and the next, and the next.

Learning to hear the 'NO' of your Noble Self is what has helped you - when you have listened. In order to hear your Noble Self's 'YES' you have to be grounded, through meditation or another means, in order to feel when joy bubbles up, when you feel a little afraid but mostly tingly in a good way, or when a calm settles into your body - this will be different for each of you.

Your Noble Self will speak to you through your body in a way unique to you. Learn what it is, how to pay attention to it when it shows up, and trust that the 'YES' is pointing to what the Universe desires for you, just as much as 'NO's" are telling you what is not for you.

What a gift to have this inner guidance system, when we learn how to tap in.

"It is an axiomatic fact that while you meditate you are speaking with your own spirit. In that state of mind you put certain questions to your spirit and the spirit answers: the light breaks forth and the reality is revealed"
-`Abdu'l-Bahá

Potential Practice

Find a quiet place and space in your life and close your eyes. Focus on your breathing until you feel centered and grounded in your body, heart, spirit, and head.

Now bring to mind something in your life where you feel alive while doing it. This could be listening to your favorite song, hiking in the woods, caring for your children, dancing, having a deep conversation with a friend, cooking, solving a problem, creating art, playing an instrument, gardening, listening to live music, writing, knitting, organizing your closets, and so on.

Whatever you bring to mind is an activity where you feel fully you. Spend time in your mind in that activity and get in touch with how you feel in your body, what emotions you feel, and what it feels like to be fully you. The more you observe yourself in this moment, the more you will begin to gather clues about how your Noble Self conveys it's 'YES' to you. Over the next few weeks begin to notice if that same 'YES' feeling shows up in your life in other activities, or when presented with a new opportunity. Over time you may find yourself changing your activities to align more and more with your 'YES'.

S E L F - A B A N D O N M E N T

Over the summer I lost sight of my personal worth. I lost sight that my most important relationship is with myself.

It felt like the last two years of rediscovering and loving myself was lost overnight. I had been working so hard on my internal growth and healing, and it felt like I had learned nothing or at least retained none of it. I was angry and felt hopeless.

At least that is how I thought I was feeling, but when I tapped in deeper, I realized I was grieving. I was grieving for having abandoned myself.

Again.

I let myself grieve. Feeling it all. Crying myself to sleep. Crying in the shower. Crying on the pages of my journal the pain of abandoning my own needs and desires yet again.

When the crying subsided, I was left with the realization that though I had abandoned myself, I still had another chance with me. I was still here waiting to be loved and adored by me.

So I worked to forgive myself for the self-abandonment and then created the most loving morning and evening routines I could imagine. I began to start and end each day loving myself and determined ways to love myself throughout the day as well.

They include dancing to my favorite music, smelling my favorite essential oils, journaling, setting an intention for the day, reading affirmations of love and enoughness about myself and my connection to the Universe, reading a lavish description of the new life I see myself living, journaling, drinking fragrant warm tea, taking a warm shower - all things that make me extremely happy as well as grounded.

And I did the routines.

Every day.

Consistency has never been my strong suit but my love for me was more important, so I stuck with them. I was feeling so good and so loved and so seen and so heard. A month in Spirit told me to add in guided meditation.

Now let me pause here. Before that moment I would have described myself as "not a meditation person". Both my Faith and my yoga practice encourage meditation, but I have always struggled to get into it.

But I followed my Spirit and today I hit a 30-day streak on the meditation app I use! And I've now added yoga into my routine as Spirit has prompted me.

I am so grateful and proud that I (re)found myself (again) and recommitted myself (again) to my relationship with me.

S P A C E

I thought that love was
a
feeling
but it's not. It's a
space
for healing
for openness
for reality
for truth
to peek its
head in
and provide the gift it's been
trying to offer our whole
lives. Sometimes we can
open up to it early in life
and sometimes
we
aren't yet ready
because love unveils all of the truth.
the parts that are sublime
and the parts that aren't and

that
requires
courage to truly see
and to truly be seen.

S TORIES

Embrace the answer you receive
because on the other side of
embracing its truth is freedom.

There is love in the Universe waiting for us to tap into it. Waiting for us to drop our walls and our barriers and our shame and our fear and our pain.

But we hold onto what we should drop because the walls, barriers, shame, fear, and pain provide us something....

What is it?

- Walls to protect ourselves – to prove that others are bad so that we can be the victim.

- Pain that feels so hard to look at but is still so comforting to nurse.

- A belief we hold that blends in with the normal/mundane understanding of society that always boils down to: My life is drama, in order to show others and myself that I am important.

- Shame that keeps us from forgiving ourselves – so that we can continue to prove to ourselves our fundamental belief that we are truly unworthy.

- Fear of trying because we may fail and prove to ourselves that we are a failure. Again.

What are you holding onto?

SELF-LOVE

"Good to say 'thank you' to the inner spirit that walks within and beside us, whispering sweet somethings in our inner ear, reminding us that we are simply, and utterly worth fighting for. We ARE simply and utterly worth fighting for."
-Jeff Brown

Self-love is an elusive and yet important skill. It is what we may refer to as self-respect but it goes much further than that. It is a gratitude for the miracle of our body, our mind, and our connection to the Divine.

Self-love is the absence of any negativity towards the self. It is about never criticizing ourselves. This may sound like not only an impossible task but also irresponsible. Many of us think that if we aren't harsh/holding ourselves to account/being critical then we will never get anything

27

done/will be lazy/will fall apart (choose whatever language applies to you). However, we have been spending our lives being self-critical and most of us are still stuck. May as well try the opposite for awhile: if it doesn't work, we can always go back to being rude to ourselves again!

Self-love is opening up the lungs of your understanding of self to breathe in your worthiness – a worthiness bestowed upon you by the Universe for simply existing.

Self-love is ACCEPTING this worthiness as being true. It is erasing all self-doubt that the Universe pays close attention to you, to you who are so special and so dear to Them. To you who are their Divine child. It is releasing it and letting it go and receiving the love of the Universe.

Self-love is building this same full-hearted, unconditional love for yourself. You are the self whom you will be with for all of eternity, so you need to learn to live with and, over time, love and cherish yourself.

Self-love requires overcoming the conditioning of a lifetime – one passed down by family, taught to you by society, and that you created in your own head. Conditioning that made you believe you are not worthy of love.

Self-love allows you to realize that being your harshest critic is not your job – society and other people do that job very well already. You are to be your biggest proponent, defender, lover, adorer, and cheerleader. You are to align yourself with and begin to exude towards yourself the love that the Universe has for you.

The Universe is so very touched by and adores you – even with, or because of, your imperfections, regrets, secrets, insecurity, and self-disregard. It wants only for you to be as happy with yourself and accepting of yourself as They are of you.

The key to Self-love is two things: It is in asking the Shadow Self to stop with the incessant self-doubting, internal criticisms, pushing us to do more and be more to please others, and the belief that playing small is safer. And it is in practicing compassionate and courageous accountability. We are not to criticize ourselves, but we are to hold ourselves to account honestly with love and compassion and justice to see where we have excelled as well as where we have fallen down. On the other side of accountability is freedom.

Your Noble Self knows - and you will begin to truly believe over time - that you are beautiful and perfect as you are including all your imperfections, that you are worthy simply for being not for what you do for others, that you are meant to play big in this world, and that the world is waiting for you to show up fully in your Truth and your Purpose.

Self-love may be the work of a lifetime or it may happen quicker – your work is to let go and accept the love of the Universe for you. And to learn how to mimic this love by speaking to yourself the way the Universe speaks to you – with nothing but love, tenderness, care, concern, rapt attention, and joy!

"All the atoms of the earth declare My love for thee."
-Bahá'u'lláh

Potential Practice

"This next week, pretend you are complete. There is no need to expect anything from yourself or to criticize or judge or change anything about you. No need to compete with anyone, no need to be more than you are (or less than you are).

"Note your experience. Notice how much pleasure, kindness, and patience you can allow yourself to have with yourself."
-Deborah Adele

EMOTIONS

Dance is a connection to myself, connection to my center, connection to the earth.

As a recovering head-only-based person, leaning into living in and feeling into the truth that is housed in my body (where the intuition lives) has been a journey I've been on for the past few years. Through an off and on yoga practice, connecting to my intuition through my body, tapping into where my emotions show up in my body as a means of feeling and releasing them, and health issues that have required me to pay closer and subtle attention to the messages of my body, I have been learning a lot.

However, it was not until I got involved in dance a little over a year ago, that my body felt fully at home and my heart opened. When dancing I feel grounded in a way I don't find anywhere else.

Today this became even more clear to me when some tough emotions came to the surface, and all I wanted to do to release them was to dance with my eyes closed to some of my favorite songs. My heart opened and my tears fell out and I felt so good and so grounded.

Where do you feel grounded?

KNOWING

In the ways of knowing
   there are many paths
   but one ending.
      So much richness in this
      world is held in
         your heart
            when you drop
               everything else
               you think you
                  know – but
                  you don't.
               So much love
                  to be shared with
                  the world when you
               do what you were put
            on this earth to do
            to love to be...be all there is.
      All that is needed exists for you
   to rise in your glory and your
   knowingness and your clarity of love.
All that is needed to be, you have.
You just need to discover it, tap into it and be.
And all will be well because it has always been so.

TRANSCENDENCE OF LIGHT

Dear
you are stronger
than you think you are
and also
stronger than
you are
in reality a flower
strong and beautiful
delicate and fragile

Oh the dichotomies of being both
strong and fragile

Where does that leave you?
In the middle

and yet
it does not

it leaves you in a

powerful
place where
the currents of
the Universe
course through you
and in you
and beyond you

You are the delicate light
that conveys the warmth
but cannot be broken

cannot be stolen

Because you are not
the light
at all

But the intricate
interplay of
light and vision
and perception
and love

and love
and love
and love

CONSPIRE

"Surrender asks us to be strong enough to engage in each moment with integrity while being soft enough to flow with the current of life."

-Deborah Adele

Be open to the promptings of the Universe. We never know where it will come from. It may be from a phone call or a book that catches the eye or a random thought seemingly plucked out of thin air.

And yet nothing is by accident, everything was/is put into place for our learning, for our understanding, for our growth.

The Universe truly, truly wants to conspire with us to make things happen. To make them happen through us. If we will only let them.

*"In showing up for **what is**, no matter how pedestrian or tedious, how aggravating or shameful, the **what is** begins to reveal itself as imbued with holiness. How do we make space in our lives for this kind of sacred seeing?"*
-Mirabai Starr

Our job is to become a clear
    channel.
          A channel so clear
               that we don't stop
                   the flow, thinking
                      if something
                         is right or
                           wrong
                    or the way we
                expected it to
          be or not to be
    or ever to be
   or that it can't possibly
be happening.

The Universe is sensitive and obedient and only wants to please. It's like water that flows. If we have a barrier, the water won't flow and instead go somewhere else where there are no barriers. No judgement at all – just an understanding that things come in their perfect Divine timing and when we release our barriers.

Love is the same way. It is always there for the taking. True, real, deep-throated, solid love, steadfast and unconditional. Ready and waiting for us to approach and bask and believe it is our birthright and the purpose of our creation.

God has *"...ordained for thy training every atom in existence and the essence of all created things."*
-Bahá'u'lláh

Potential Practice

Spend time getting in touch with yourself by sitting somewhere and focusing on your breathing. Ask yourself this simple question: 'Who am I?', and be open and curious to see what you hear. If you hear I am a friend, ask to go deeper. If you hear I am a parent, ask to go deeper. If you hear I am a spouse, ask to go deeper. If you hear I am my job, ask to go deeper. If you hear I am a baker/dancer/skier (or whatever your favorite hobby is), ask to go deeper.

You are not denying that you are a friend or a parent or a spouse or that you have that job or those hobbies. What you are asking for is who you are, past the roles you are for others and past the ways you occupy your time.

You are listening for the Truth of who you are. You may hear: I am light, I am connected, I am happy, I am protection, I am love, I am guided, or whatever else your Noble Self wants you to know about them and you. You may not hear much at first but trust you will hear over time.

Return to this practice often to listen.

Shadow Self

"Anyone who perceives his shadow and his light simultaneously sees himself from two sides and thus gets the middle."

-Carl Jung

Our Shadow Self has been our constant companion and has protected us throughout our lives. Your Shadow Self may be a feisty fighter who will defend you verbally or physically at the drop of a hat. Your Shadow Self may be a controlling creature, working diligently to ensure that everything is planned for in advance, is perfect, and is always on point to defend against anyone's criticisms. Your Shadow Self may be a benign being, who plays it cool like nothing impacts them and just going with the flow but always seeking the small corners of the world where they can hide. Your Shadow Self may be an engaging entity always working to please others, avoid conflict, and seek approval as a way to ensure their safety. Or your Shadow Self may be a combination, showing up as a controlling creature at work and an engaging entity with friends and family or a benign being until pushed and then will show up as a feisty fighter.

Our Shadow Self was created when we were a child. When we looked around our environment and determined how to survive and get attention and love. We decided what would work for us as a five-year old and it worked – you are reading this book because they helped you get to adulthood. However, as adults we need more than just survival or attention – we need to learn how to thrive and to live our Truth and Purpose. We need to learn how to strengthen and listen to our Noble Self. And we need to learn how to get the Shadow Self to work on our behalf with our Noble Self to align to our Truth and Purpose.

Many people have been taught - if they learned they had an ego self or Shadow Self at all - that this lower self is a part to be shunned and ignored. In fact it is the opposite – the Shadow Self is our roommate no matter what, so it is much better to make friends with it, understand it, and embrace it.

The Shadow Self stayed at the ages it was created – around five or six years old. It has the emotional intelligence and patience of a five-year old, which is to say: not much. And yet it also has the innocence and willingness to please of a five or six year old who just wants to be loved and listened to. It is prone to tantrum, to sabotage our lives and relationships, and to blame others to believe itself to be the victim if it is not given proper attention.

So we listen.

But just because we listen doesn't mean we follow its advice. In fact we should not. A five-year old should not be guiding the life of an adult. But we can listen to it and embrace its intention to try to be helpful, while letting the Noble Self make the decisions.

H E A L I N G

Tonight my daughter was playing with a candle and lighting a little bit of paper towel to watch it burn. She was being super safe but the smell hit me in that moment and I remembered the experience of escaping a smoke-filled burning building - a memory that happened 13 years ago and really didn't impact me much back then.

I thought.

I had stored that memory and the trauma and fear that I suppressed feeling back then (I am always the calm one in the face of trauma), and here it was coming to light.

But there was more.

That fear brought up a feeling of fear and terror I had on a trip to the Grand Canyon years ago. A feeling that I had suppressed to just make it through the experience then. A person I trusted with my daughter's safety (my daughter was 8 or so at the time) put her repeatedly in harm's way by having her very close to the edge of the canyon where there were no guardrails. The more I requested the behavior to stop, the more it continued. And the more it continued, the more my body was literally doubled over in terror and fear (those with children will understand this bodily response when we fear for our children).

At the time I didn't have the space or time to process through it, and now I'm processing through that feeling of fear and terror. The fear and terror came from not being in control. And I am so grateful that these feelings are coming up.

Finally.

My response to trauma, as I mentioned before, has been to be calm. That is how I've always been and that is how I continue to be in stressful situations. No emotions. Just calm. And no emotions in this kind of situation is as problematic as having debilitating emotions would be. So I am so grateful to have finally tapped in.

For many years I shied away from my emotions, being scared that they would overtake me. That I wouldn't know what to do with the mess if I really let them out and felt them. But when I finally did let them out, I realized that they aren't the scary boogie monsters I made them out to be.

They were actually a message that I needed to listen to and feel. In many cases only moments were needed to truly feel them and then they disappeared, relieved that they were finally heard.

Emotions are messages, each one. When I cry when I'm sad the message is that I feel like I lost something I loved. When I am angry the anger is the message to me that something felt unjust or unfair. When I am disappointed the message is that I feel like something did not meet my expectations. When I am happy the message is that something is bringing me joy.

When an emotion comes up it is not important to do anything but feel them.

Determining whether I actually lost something or something was unjust or didn't meet my expectations, or that something actually did bring me joy is still an important step. But this is separate from the emotions themselves that just need to be felt first.

This is why it is important that we don't tell ourselves or others (even though it's habit for many of us) "don't cry" or "don't be angry". Feel the messages, feel the emotions, and then figure the rest out. It takes a lot of work to learn the skills to do this, but the work has been so worth it for me.

So here I am with emotions finally opening up, and I am so grateful!!

S E A R C H

There is a love so deep so
great
that there is no reason to
search anymore.

There is a peace
so great that
nothing else
exists.

Love just is and there is no need to struggle.

Anymore.

You are worthy
to accept it
not for
anything, any great
deed but
just
because you
exist.

He/She/They chose to create you
and you are here to be loved.

Eternally.

Your job
is to love yourself as God/The Universe
loves you.

It is all simple
And yet so very complex.

And here we are at the beginning
and the end
at the same time.

U N I V E R S A L I T Y

Being in full freedom is the greatest gift of all.

We are one with all that is. This has always been the case and always will be.

Ours is to remember this and merge again with the oneness that exists.

What keeps us out of this oneness are our own feelings of unworthiness, loss, disconnection, abandonment, and fear. What allows us to access it is dropping those things and finally letting it in.

There is nothing else to do but just be. And being in full freedom is the greatest gift of all.

Never Fades

She knows who she is
        and with joy
                she lives that
                        and others feel
                                a little more
                                        real.

She knows what it feels like to be confined
        and she wears her freedom like a pin
                to remind her
                of what she has
                        and of what she has left behind.

                      It has been years now
                      and yet the sharpness of that
freedom
                          never fades.

RELEASE

Truly trusting the Universe means that I can FINALLY truly relax and release.

I have not been truly letting go and letting the Universe handle things for awhile.

This is hard to admit to myself.

I was looking through my bookshelf today for a new journal and ran into a card that said "God, I don't get this, but You've got this" and I realized that it didn't resonate for me the same way it had when I bought it last summer in a card shop. The message makes sense for sure but the feeling that it truly represents where I am right now, that I TRULY trust that the Universe has this and I can trust Their Will?

Not so much.

Perfect time for reflection and I thank the Universe for putting this card in my path today. I GET that the Universe sends me messages. I look for them every day. And I know they are there whether I see them or not. But I realize that I don't truly trust the Universe in a real way.

I have in the past and They pulled me through SO many things. But it's not where I am now.

A close friend of mine has told me what has helped her is to remember to relax and release into reliance on the Universe. Trusting the Universe is one thing (and not easy by any stretch). But relaxing and releasing into reliance on Them is a whole other thing.

For me trust feels like a head thing, a mental acknowledgement that something/someone will do as they say they will. Reliance feels like a body thing, I rely on my heart to pump and my lungs to breathe. Relying on the Universe is a bodily knowing that They will always be there just like our heart and lungs.

That is huge.

And I can feel how amazing it would be to have that reliance, that true knowing that They have this. That They are holding us in Their arms and I am safe. That They love me and only wants the best for me, in fact has in store for me more than I can ever hope for myself if I'd let Them do Their work and get out of the way. The amazing life I live now is a testament to Their Work. And yet it is so easy to slip into "I'VE got this".

Truly relying on Them means that I can FINALLY truly relax and release. Relax my brain and my hyper alertness to danger that I have had for a lifetime. Release the tension in my shoulders and my lower back and my forehead from overthinking.

Relax and release into reliance on the Universe feels like getting into a hot bath after a long day.

Like taking a long deep breath of air in the middle of the woods.

Like hearing the waves on the ocean while sitting in the sun.

Like listening to the babbling of a stream while sitting on its sun dappled shores.

Like hearing my favorite song and dancing to it with my eyes closed.

Like putting on my favorite outfit and the feel of the clothes against my skin.

Like the smell of my favorite meal cooked by close friends or family.

It feels like those moments when I know all is well. Even for that moment.

Relaxing and releasing into reliance is trusting and believing that these are not just moments. That I can tap into that feeling always because the Universe doesn't just have this, They have me. They want me to always have that feeling of Comfort in every moment. It is only when I believe myself independent or separate from Them, from all that is, that I think I can do this thing called life on my own, that I don't feel this Comfort.

It's only when I let my Shadow Self tell me that I'm not worthy of feeling comfort, that I don't feel this Comfort. It's only when I let the busyness of life pull me away, that I don't feel this Comfort. It's only when I focus on what isn't working in my life, that I don't feel this Comfort. The old saying "it's not you, it's me" holds true. The Universe is always there, it is just me who has pulled away. Their Comfort is always there - it is just me who has deprived myself.

I need to take those steps. I need to remember that They have a greater plan for me than I can ever imagine. I need to believe that I am worthy. I need to remember with gratitude all that the Universe has given me in my life so far. I need to open myself up to the hot bath and the sound of the ocean and the smell of my favorite food and the feeling of dancing to my favorite song and rest and relax in Their arms where I was made to be.

And so I will.

CREATIVITY

I was allowed to be an observer to the process, once again finding my flow and my zone and me.

As a child I was never far away from some art materials. Drawing, painting, coloring. I did it without thinking, without wondering why or what it meant. I liked to do it and it felt like a natural extension of myself. This continued on through middle school where I also picked up the habit of journaling. I don't remember deciding to journal - thinking through my feelings and ideas through writing came naturally to me. And because I was writing it was in my journal that no one else would read, I felt comfortable with exploration and depth and play and fluidity of language.

I could spend hours doing either activity and feeling fully refreshed and in touch with myself. At the time I didn't think about what I was doing, but looking back I realize that it was my zone (where we feel the most aligned, the most alive and the most grounded).

I continued with art in high school and while I still enjoyed it, it became about a product, a result, creating something with meaning and a message. I took on the stories from society that something isn't Important if it's not productive, if it doesn't mean something, if it isn't a Thing to be seen, understood, and valued by others.

I continued with art, but I lost touch with the zone of creativity, the play of getting lost in it all, the exploration of the materials and what they could create on the page. Instead, I was concerned with the result and began comparing myself with others, began being conscious of my work as seen by others rather than an activity that I let myself get lost in. What kept me grounded to myself was my continual journaling. My ability to articulate my inner life and my inner thoughts and my learnings continued and developed.

When I went to college, I decided to take a break from art and focus on academics. I expected it to be a short hiatus as I explored another side of me through my economics and international studies degrees at a liberal arts college. I loved the learning, I loved the mind opening, I loved my classmates, and that was my zone. I continued to journal and write regularly throughout college as I continued to develop.

I got married soon after college, and in my youth and the dynamics of the relationship I didn't create space to return to my art and I journaled only off and on.

As a result I lost touch with me. I allowed my life to be about us, and less about me. We had our daughter and it was an even greater us, but I let myself be written out of the equation.

There were moments would I feel the zone that came over when I created art – coloring with my daughter, making art for her, painting with my dad when he was in art therapy for his brain tumor that eventually took his life. There were moments I would feel the zone that came over when I wrote – times that I made space to journal, when I wrote social media posts about my experiences with my dad as he was passing and what a transformative experience that was for me. These posts were so cathartic for me and was the first time I'd shared my writing widely. I didn't intend to share my writing but to share my experiences, but the feedback I received was that it touched others in a meaningful way. It was my first inkling that I could touch people through writing, but at the time I wasn't paying attention to that.

Since my divorce a few years ago, I have spent time getting back to myself. Through journaling. Through coaching and therapy. Through healing. Through learning and relationships. Through re-finding what I love to do, how I love to be, how I express myself. Who I am. Through letting go and listening to my long silenced Noble Self again. Through letting go of perfectionism. Through listening to guidance I began receiving from the Universe. I began to share some of these experiences on social media through my writing. I began sharing the raw side of my experiences as a way of leaning into letting go of perfectionism. Again I felt like I was sharing, I didn't see it as sharing my writing, but again I received feedback that what I was saying and how I was saying it was touching them.

A friend of mine invited me to an open mic event for her birthday a few years ago. It was a milestone birthday and she had decided to push herself out of her comfort zone by writing a poem to read at the open mic. I felt inspired to support her by doing the same thing.

Now, up until then I had never written a poem outside of an English class. In fact I'd never really gotten into poetry as a reader. But I decided to support her so I gave it a try and even got up the nerve to read it. And I found afterwards that sometimes in my journaling my thoughts came out as poems. I found the experience interesting but just one more way of exploring myself in my journals.

In a conversation, my sister told me that she had always thought of me as a writer, and I remember being blown away. "Wait, I'm not a writer, I just write things. I journal, I put words together when I need to. That's not a writer." But I thought about it some, I let it gestate for a while, I let it roll around in my brain. I processed through why I couldn't take on the title of writer. I felt like a writer was someone who wrote short stories or novels, who identified as a writer, who were good at writing. I love reading novels but have no interest in writing one, therefore I'm not a writer. At least these were the conclusions my mind came to.

But I received her seeing of me and took it on for size. I realized over time, gradually that I was a writer of experiences, of reality, and of poetry. Writing is where I have always brought order to my thoughts but also where I open up to inspiration beyond me. It comes out as poems, as social media posts, as weekly writings for my private coaching clients.

My process for writing this book has been to ask each of the things I have written over the past few years to tell me if they want to be included and in what order. In my ability to hear my Noble Self now, I have found that I can hear other things that want to speak to me like my art and my writing.

I asked my work to come together, and they assembled themselves in front of me in a way that my brain could have never logically organized with such depth and simplicity.

Simultaneous to writing this book over these past few months, I knew it was time to tap back into my artistic side. A dear friend was holding a class on exploring creativity and the creative process and it was an immediate 'YES'. I joined the first art class I'd taken since high school decades before. I was me but I was also so very different. I consciously took the skills I had learned over the years about how to let go of perfectionism, about how to be open to guidance, about not worrying about the end result but the process itself. I reminded myself of the zone and the flow that creativity was and always has been for me. In the 6-week course I let myself make marks on a page that to my mind felt incomplete or unfinished, outside of my comfort zone, but I continued to let my art and my heart tell me exactly what to do. I leaned into letting the art be what it wanted to be. I leaned into listening to what it wanted me to do, and I was allowed to be an observer to the process, once again finding my flow and my zone and me. One of my first art pieces after decades of not accessing that side of my creativity appears on this cover of this book, and I am grateful for the reconnection to myself through it.

Money

What I didn't expect to experience was the level of freedom that came from authentic and loving accountability.

My relationship with money throughout my life has been complicated. Growing up, our family didn't have much money but lived in a very affluent area, which created embarrassment for me in school when I didn't have the right clothes or the same lifestyle as everyone else. Like many families, we never talked about money, but all I knew was we didn't have much left at the end of the month. My learned behavior of not asking for my own needs already created in an unhealthy family dynamic, was exacerbated by lack of financial resources. I learned to not want much and believed it was my truth, not one created by circumstances.

I got married right after college and worked with my then husband to create a financial life based on incomplete understandings we both brought in about how to handle money. Early on when we both had entry-level jobs that didn't pay much, instead of living within our means we managed to stack up debt. We both grew up without much, and credit made it too easy to create a life borrowing against our future and subconsciously compensating for what we didn't have in our past. We would cycle in and out of debt and I can't tell you the number of times that I would cash out a retirement account to pay off debt or my then husband would sell a car he had bought for cheap and fixed up to do the same.

We had an underlying belief that as soon as money would come in it would leave. And what we believed was our reality. We didn't expect to retire with much (what we learned from our families), and a decade into our marriage we were making that expectation a reality. This reactive stance towards life shown in how we responded to money, and was also reflected in many other areas of our life, including our careers where we felt stuck in dead end jobs even with our college degrees.

I can't remember the impetus - maybe it was the arrival of our daughter and the fact that, even though I had planned to, we couldn't financially swing it for me to be a stay-at-home mom like I hoped for - or it was the boom and bust cycle of my then husband's business that created a rocky financial foundation - but I knew I needed to start learning to be proactive in my career to make a stable income in a job I enjoyed, making a difference.

Over a period of 4-5 years I did a lot of internal work to learn how to determine what I wanted at work. I realized I deserved to be powerful and how to use my voice, did a ton of soul searching to determine what my skills were (a lot of soft skills in a hard-skill-focused business world - that I began to understand were the most difficult and some of the most important and they came to me naturally), and went back to school to get my MBA. I was in my early 30s at this point and felt like I was so behind my friends in both career and financial goals, but I kept moving forward. I retooled my entire career from financial services to change management/organization development consulting, and with the help of lots of mentors I began to thrive and excel. Each job moved me up career wise and financially and I was proud of who I was becoming.

But our beliefs about money didn't change. We still believed we wouldn't retire with much, that whenever we had money it would leave. Even when I was making more money, our negative beliefs were still creating a cycle of debt.

Sadly, it was around this time that my marriage ended - the growth I had put in around my career was spreading to other parts of my life as I was realizing I did have needs and worth and a voice, and I hit a crossroads where that growth no longer included my then husband.

Fortunately, I was financially in a place where I could support myself well as a single mother (I am so aware of what a privilege this is and I will forever be grateful). In the divorce we split the debt but each kept our own student loans. In the year after the divorce, I set up a new home with furnishings which added to my debt.

I've spent the past few years since the divorce (re)discovering myself and what I want and need and enjoy and truly embracing my worth and my me-ness fully. This included spending money on what brought me joy after so many years without, including dance and travel and inner healing classes/coaching.

And yet still what had not changed was my relationship and understanding of money. Even with making more money I did not believe that I would retire well, and that money would always leave right when I'd get it. Again: reality was matching my beliefs (they always do).

So this year it was finally time to tackle this part of my life. I finally unearthed the beliefs that had been running me throughout. I began to transform my thinking about money from scarcity to abundance, from passivity to proactivity.

Through further study and conversations with friends I started to understand the sacredness of being a good steward of money and looked at how to stick to a budget as a form of freedom, not captivity. I started watching YouTube videos about FIRE (financial independence retire early) and learned about living below one's means, the math behind compound interest and investing wisely and the magic of time. I did a TON of number crunching and stuck to bare-bones budgets. I finally got my emergency fund to a reasonable level (though still below the 3-6 month's worth of expenses level that it should be at) and started pummeling my debt.

Through all of this, what I didn't expect to experience was the level of freedom that came from authentic accountability. I finally knew where every dollar was going, I was making choices based on my future self and what it would feel like to be out from under the weight of debt (since I entered college at 18, I have never been without debt – more than two decades is a long time to carry that weight). I began a loving relationship with money for the first time. I began to realize that my financial life didn't have to be a drudgery of counting every penny or ignoring it (the two extremes I would swing between) but rather an interchange of energy.

The affirmation I wrote for myself earlier this year to pull towards me the reality of what I wanted was: "I am allowing money to come in and play in my world and be used/shared where it is drawn to. I am the trustee and money knows where it wants to be. It is so exciting to fund my dreams and my hopes, and I know that I will become financially independent (debt free) in 2021. The weightlessness this has given me is indescribable."

Until I wrote this I did not think of money as being playful or an energy that gets excited to help us, and yet that is how it came to me to be experienced, and I began the process to see it that way.

At the time of writing this affirmation I did not know how getting out of debt in 2021 would be possible, but I worked through the steps to manifest it in my life (believing it to be true, thanking the Universe for making it true, and then turning it over to watch in fascination for it to come into being through obeying the promptings of intuition for the next right thing to do).

And now, today, at the end of 2020, I have achieved the goal I asked the Universe to make happen: I am completely debt free. Not only did it come to be, but ahead of schedule. The Universe truly conspires to help us when we know what we want. God is Great. All of the time.

I am so very grateful for what has gotten me to this point. All the learning and growth and setbacks and guidance and the right ideas at the right time. And those who have been on this journey with me and who have inspired me or listened to me or said the exact thing I needed to hear.

MANIFESTING

"It is seldom as simple as asking the Universe for what we want and we get it. We need to get our emotional world consistent with our requests before they will be taken seriously by the Universe. The more emotionally unresolved we are, the denser the message we transmit. The trick is to clear ourselves from the inside-out so that we are emanating from a clear and unified channel. Then our request might carry more weight, then it might fall on open ears."

-Jeff Brown

Your mind is a powerful tool that directly impacts the world that you live in. If you focus on lack, difficulties, and self-criticism, you will notice those more often; if you focus on gratitude and abundance you will also notice these more often. The vibration you operate at will match the things you think about all the time, so it is important to choose what you think about. Negative thoughts vibrate at low frequencies, positive thoughts vibrate at higher frequencies. The goal is not to banish all negative thoughts and focus only on the positive – in fact that is very unhealthy. It is about raising your vibration to be equal to the things that you really want in life. If you want a happy life, in the job of your dreams, with a partner who supports you, in a loving community where you are growing from learning new things, you have to vibrate at the level of that type of life.

One key way to do this is through meditation and manifesting by following these steps:

1. **Desire:** Ground yourself through meditation, deep breathing, listening to soothing music, walking in nature, or whatever makes you feel in touch with your Noble Self. Write what you desire and be as detailed as possible. What you desire could be about a specific part of your life or your life holistically, it could be in the short-, medium-, or long-term. Write it in the present tense and in addition to details write about how attaining your desire has impacted your life, how it has allowed you to be, and what it has allowed you to do.

2. **Feeling:** When you are done writing it, read your updated desire to yourself as if you are living it now. How does it feel? What emotions are you experiencing? Let your head and your heart and your body and your soul connect to those feelings. Now write those feelings as "I am" statements, for instance "I am excited", "I am centered", etc.

3. **Gratitude:** Now spend time being truly grateful, from the bottom of your heart, soul, mind and body, for feeling this way, for getting you to your desire. Be grateful to yourself, to your past that were all steppingstones, to your support system/community, to the Divine/the Universe/nature. Sit in this gratitude for a while – just enjoy.

4. **Release:** Trust that your desires will manifest exactly how they are supposed to and when they are supposed to. This is the hardest step because our cynical/practical minds want to either tell us how impossible attaining our desire is, or they tell us that we can't possibly get to our desire without a detailed plan that we work on assiduously. We need to stay away from both things. We need to trust that the Universe will make this happen and if we doubt or try to control it through a plan we create, it will not happen with ease.

5. **Raise your Vibration:** For every "I am" statement you listed in #2 think of things you do or could do

now that make you feel this way. These things will be small and don't have to be related to your desire. So, for instance if one of your feeling statements was "I am excited", think about what you can do now that gets you excited. For instance, if dancing makes you excited, be sure to do more of it. Do this for each feeling statement and then add these things into your regular routine. The goal here is to raise your vibrations to the same level as how you will feel when your desire is manifested. This will serve as a homing beacon for the vibration of your desire to find your equal vibration when it is time to manifest.

6. **Affirmation:** Read your Desire from step one each day. Be sure to do so with trust and without letting doubt come into your head, heart, body, or soul. This may be hard at first but over time reading your desire and focusing on trust will become easier.

7. **Celebrate:** Celebrate each day. Celebrate on days when you see things show up in your life as a result of your manifesting and on days when you don't. The Universe is making things happen whether you see it or not. And YOU are always a reason to celebrate, so be sure to do this daily. When you have manifested what you desire, celebrate even bigger and continue onto your next goal.

TEARS

What a gift we are given in tears

I am a huge believer in letting the tears flow for release now rather than dealing with a repressed version later. Tears are such a healer and an indication of where we are in our journey – the happy parts and the harder parts.

I cried tears of relief/healing/joy just this afternoon as I was driving. I realized that something I had been learning about myself recently put something from my past into an entirely different light, and that made me grateful for a past I hadn't always been so happy about.

I arrived at my destination before I had a chance to fully feel through the tears to allow them to cleanse my heart.

When I got a moment this evening I went back to that same mental/heart space to finish the process and the feeling of relief and freedom I got was indescribable.

What a gift we are given in tears.

SUPPORTIVE UNIVERSE

"And, when you want something, all the Universe conspires in helping you to achieve it."
-Paulo Coelho

An amazing thing has happened from trusting in the Universe and opening up to possibilities.

About a month ago I got a call from an old friend, whom I hadn't talked to in years, saying she had a job that I may be interested in. I was in a space of mindfulness and connection and openness to things coming my way in case they are for me, so I responded.

I was not looking for a job and in fact I really enjoyed my work, I had assembled a great team doing valuable work for our client who loved and trusted us, we were awaiting news on the award of a renewal of our contract and were very confident we would get it, and I loved my boss and my company. So in summary: very happy. I started through a series of interviews just to see where it would go. The job sounded intriguing but would have been a lateral move.

A week or so after I started the interview process with my friend's company, we start getting indications at my job that we possibly did NOT get the renewal of the contract, which surprised all of us.

I realized that the job opportunity came in time for a need I didn't even know I had. And I had to pause in gratitude.

How MANY times do things come my way that I passed up because I didn't know I needed it until it wasn't there. Thankfully this time, because I was reconnected to me and the Divine (and therefore my intuition), I was able to respond to what was coming my way.

And it was answering a prayer I hadn't even asked!! A need I didn't even know that I had!!

I'm in deep awe at this and so very blessed to realize that the Universe truly wants only what is best for us, even when sometimes we ourselves don't know what it is.

This past week we got official notice at work that our contract did not get renewed (Thankfully I was not losing my job but what my new work would be was uncertain), AND I got the offer letter for the new job.

All on the same day.

Everything for us is always on time. Every time.

I am humbled and grateful for a conspiratorial and supportive Universe.

G ROUNDEDNESS

Groundedness is about connecting to our bodies where our Noble Self lives.

The Noble Self is connected to the Divine as well as to our bodies, so it is through connecting with grounding into our bodies that we connect to Ourselves.

Our minds live in the past or the future. Our hearts live mostly in the past. Our bodies are the only thing that lives in the present always, and so it is what we need to connect to.

This groundedness starts with our breath – with centering our thoughts on it and focusing on breathing deeper and releasing tension we are holding in our bodies.

It continues with connecting to gratitude for what our bodies do for us every day. Breathing without needing to think about it, eating and digesting food, allowing us to walk around the earth. Our bodies are amazing machines that function so beautifully.

It continues through letting our thoughts cross our mind and lovingly letting them flit by. We could also use the time in groundedness for asking our Noble Self what they believe about the thought or any advice they have and listening to what is shared.

Groundedness is not about trying to escape ourselves but about connecting to our bodies where our Noble Self lives.

L O V E

You find that healing looks like more love.

Love is everything. There is nothing without love. It starts with loving the self, the whole self: the Noble Self and the Shadow Self; the highs and the lows; the things that we celebrate and the things that we cringe about.

All things are for our purpose and for our path and when we stay conscious and continue to love even when it's hard, we continue to live.

Without love there is no life.

But there are days, weeks, months, years where this can feel hopeless. Where we don't feel love. Where we don't feel life.

Maybe we are in a toxic relationship, or estranged from family, or in a dead-end job, or in a series of failed relationships leaving us more desolate than the last. Maybe we play out the same internal struggle where our Shadow Self reminds us of how unworthy we are, of how we are only and always truly alone, of how we are unloved, of how everything that has happened in our lives is our fault, and maybe at the lowest points how pointless this all is.

The hardest thing in the world, and I say this without exaggeration, is to pick up the shambles of your internal life and begin the process of loving yourself.

Maybe it's finally getting out of bed. Maybe it's closing the laptop at the end of the day even though there is more work that could be done. Maybe it's remembering to go for a walk in the sun even when you don't feel like it. Maybe it's going to bed on time. Maybe it's saying no to a request from someone in order to make time to care for yourself. Maybe it's speaking your truth. Maybe it's not believing the criticisms or belittling or undermining or manipulations from others, even for a moment. Maybe it's whatever you need to feel loved, in even the smallest way in the smallest moment.

These small moments build up a feeling of love, and your Noble Self and Shadow Self begin to feel your love. And they begin to love you back.

Your Noble Self begins to respond by slowly, quietly sharing more of their wisdom and guidance with you because they are beginning to trust that you will listen. And in your growing love for yourself, you do. They tell you to rest and you do. They tell you to call a friend you haven't thought of in a while and you do and it's the exact conversation you needed to have in that moment. They inspire you on a project for work you've been struggling with and you listen and make more progress than you thought possible. They remind you to pause and put your face to the sun when you are rushing to get to work and you do.

Your Shadow Self begins to slow down the criticisms. They

are less quick to judge yourself and others. They become a bit less fearful because they are beginning to trust that you will listen. And in your growing love for yourself, you do.

Your Shadow Self tells you that you aren't worthy, and in your love you hear the pain behind that and you feel into what it feels like to feel unworthy and you love yourself even more. They tell you that you are just going to screw up this project, just like you always do, and in your love you hear the fear behind that and you feel into what it feels like to be afraid and you love yourself even more. They tell you your partner doesn't love you, and in your love you hear the pain behind that and you feel into what it feels like to feel unloved and you love yourself even more.

So in your growing love, your Shadow Self continues to quiet down and your Noble Self continues to grow in confidence. And your Noble Self begins to guide you on how to heal the emotional pain and hurt that your body has been carrying around. And your Noble Self begins to guide you on how to continue to heal your relationship with yourself, with your family, with your friends, and with the world. Your Noble Self has the wisdom of the Divine that they are learning more and more to share with you, and you are learning more and more to trust.

You find that healing looks like more love.

This love shows up as gratitude for how strong you are to make it through the hard things you've been through. This love shows up as gratitude for those who stayed at your side to support you and those that left, because both were blessings. This love shows up as gratitude to the Universe for getting you this far. This love shows up as gratitude for where you are right now in this moment, even if your past moments have been difficult. This love shows up as gratitude for what you have learned.

This love shows up as full accountability for your actions that have created the life you have lived and are living. This love shows up as full accountability for times when you have hurt others. This love shows up as full accountability for times when you have allowed yourself to be hurt by others. This love shows up as full accountability for times when you have hurt yourself.

This love shows up as full accountability for when you have abandoned your loved ones. This love shows up as full accountability for when you have allowed yourself to be abandoned by others. This love shows up as full accountability for when you have abandoned yourself.

This love shows up as full accountability for when you haven't loved others. This love shows up as full accountability for when you have allowed others not to love you. This love shows up as full accountability for when you haven't loved yourself.

This love shows up as full forgiveness for everyone, especially yourself, who hurt or was hurt.

This love shows up as full forgiveness for everyone, especially yourself, who abandoned or was abandoned.

This love shows up as full forgiveness for everyone, especially yourself, who didn't love or wasn't loved.

This love shows up as fully feeling all the emotions through the process of gratitude, full accountability and forgiveness. You must feel your feelings. All of them. Every one. Whenever they show up.

Fully feeling all the emotions is your healing, it is your

freedom.

Your body will only give you the amount of emotions that you can handle, so trust it. You will not break if you feel the emotions, even though it feels like you might.

Take the time to feel your emotions, hear what they need to tell you, and then let them go.

Take the time to feel your emotions, hear what they need to tell you, and then let them go.

Take the time to feel your emotions, hear what they need to tell you, and then let them go.

Do this as many times as you may need.

It may be useful to journal as you feel, listen to, and let go of these emotions. Or speak out loud what is coming up as you feel, listen to, and let go of these emotions. Or to listen to or move to music with the same emotional depth to them as you feel, listen to, and let go of these emotions. Or to run or exercise as you feel, listen to, and let go of these emotions. Or be in nature as you feel, listen to, and let go of these emotions.

The emotions may come in waves, or they may come at random moments, or they may overtake you all at one time. This process may take minutes or hours or days or weeks or months or years. Let it be how your body needs it to be.[1]

---

[1] Note: If you are prone to depressive or particularly negative thoughts, set an alarm. Feel the emotions full out until the alarm goes off. That way you can trust that you won't get stuck in them. Plan for what to do after the timer goes off to bring

In this process you will hear messages from your emotions. You may begin to understand that you fear being abandoned, that you still have feelings of unworthiness, that you don't feel like you are successful enough, that you are ashamed of something in your past, that you struggle to exercise because you don't trust your body, that you are feeling lifeless in your job, that you have the same unhealthy relationship with different partners, that you don't feel like you are living an authentic life, or whatever else that shows up for you.

What you are learning is what needs additional attention to heal, and in your love for yourself you seek assistance. Depending on the nature of the issue you may want to seek out a trusted psychiatrist, psychologist, therapist, coach, pastor, rabbi, religious leader, counselor, traditional healer, or wise trusted friend who can keep your confidences and whom you wholeheartedly trust. Or you search out books to read, courses to take, or thought leaders to follow on social media to help you work through what needs healing.

And you begin to find freedom. And peace. And internal calm. And more things to heal. And more gratitude. And more accountability. And more forgiveness. And more freedom. And more peace. And more internal calm. And more things to heal...

The freedom is love.

---

you back up if you are worried you need help getting back out of the darkness. Maybe a walk or a shower or a conversation with a friend. Also if you are working with a therapist make sure to talk with them before doing this.

The peace is love.
The internal calm is love.
The healing is love.

The freedom is life.
The peace is life.
The internal calm is life
The healing is life.

AFTER THOUGHTS

When I embarked on this writing I knew my Shadow Self would pop up and tell me to stop.

I've been confronted with feelings of not wanting to be this open, this vulnerable. I have a story in my head that I have to be perfect (oldest daughter, trying to cover for my embarrassment of family issues, and other reasons) and this pops up when I try to share that things are hard or I don't know what to do.

I have been working to quiet my Shadow Self that tells me that I have to be perfect. The voice that tells me that if I'm not perfect no one will love me (even though I have so much proof that this is not true: I am not perfect and I have so many people who love me unconditionally). So, when I embarked on this writing I knew the Shadow Self would pop up and tell me to stop and I knew that it was the right time in my journey to do this.

I started sharing some of my very vulnerable writing on social media, and my Shadow Self started telling me that I shouldn't have shared my difficulties. That I was being too open. I contemplated deleting the post. But then I took some deep breaths and I started to read the responses and I saw how much what I was saying resonated with people.

My Shadow Self popped up a few times while I was reading the responses. Especially when someone would give me advice, my Shadow Self would say "see they think you are broken, they are telling you how to fix you. I told you this was a bad idea" and I would listen and then tell her I didn't want to take her advice but appreciated her concern.

And then I remembered what a friend told me recently: after you share something huge it is normal to have a vulnerability hangover where you regret it all and want to take it all back. So instead I kept reading. And I saw messages from people who didn't want to respond publicly because they were struggling deeply and appreciated me sharing.

And then I started sharing my poems and my Shadow Self would pop up and tell me to pull back into the safety of being perfect. To stop being out there. In response, I began sharing my artwork because I see that sharing is my growth edge (the place where I know there is growth but it scares me to death).

And so I chose to pull everything together into a book even though my Shadow Self is telling me I'm not a writer. I chose to do it anyway because my Noble Self knows the

Truth of who I am and the Purpose for which I was created, and so I share myself with more people.

Invitation

If what was shared here resonates with you and you want to be part of a community of people who are learning together how to follow our Noble Selves to live our unique Truth and Purpose, join us by following us on:

- **Follow Your Design Official Book Group** on Facebook

- **follow_your_design_rediscovery** page on Instagram

For more information including about our courses on (re)discovering your Purpose and Truth, retreats, blogs/articles/videos or private coaching sessions with Michelle Layli Farnsworth check out our website www.mainspringfoundations.com.

About the Author

Michelle Layli Farnsworth is learning to call herself an artist, writer, coach, facilitator, instructor, pattern maker, learner and explorer of inner life. Her organization Mainspring Foundations is dedicated to creating community and personal transformation through courses, retreats, books and private coaching sessions. She lives with her daughter in Washington, DC.

G r a t i t u d e

I'd like to thank my parents Lynn and Craig for being searchers after inner truth in their own very human ways. I began my search for Purpose and Truth early because of them.

I'd like to thank my sister Leah, for so much, but specifically for being a mirror to me, to show me I am a writer. For that I will be eternally grateful.

I am grateful for Renee Timberlake for our lifelong friendship (though I got here first!), never-ending and exuberant support of me always; Rich Hwang for his long friendship and encouragement when I was a vulnerable new poet; for Krista Dragomer who has been with me for my creative journey since middle school and now upon my return; for Alison Koeppel for hours and hours of conversations and your insightful questions that helped me hone my thinking; for Carlos Miller for truly seeing me before I could see myself; for the many friends over the years who have told me how much my writing has resonated with them; for Scarlet Fitzgerald and our queenly sisterhood, who with her vision brought about so much transformation in our lives; for Carlisa Jacobs who in her dreaming big has raised me up to dream even bigger; and for my daughter Karida for her wisdom and clarity and for choosing me.

And finally, but most importantly I am grateful to the Universe, God, and all that is for using me as a mouthpiece to share your Love. I am humbled and blessed.

References

Below is a list of books that I have quoted from:

Power v Force
David R. Hawkins, M.D., Ph.D.

Paris Talks
`Abdu'l-Bahá

Love it Forward
Jeff Brown

Gleanings
Bahá'u'lláh

The Yamas & Niyamas: Exploring Yoga's Ethical Practice
Deborah Adele

Wild Mercy: Living the Fierce and Tender Wisdom
of the Women Mystics
Mirabai Starr

The Hidden Words
Bahá'u'lláh

Good and Evil in Analytical Psychology
Carl Jung

The Alchemist
Paulo Coelho

CPSIA information can be obtained
at www.ICGtesting.com
Printed in the USA
JSHW040251160421
13629JS00003B/21